Like. A. Phoenix.

The Elevation Of The One Self.

Z.N.X NATALLANNI

13TH & JOAN

For permission requests, write to the publisher, addressed "Attention: Permissions Coordinator," 205 N. Michigan Avenue, Suite #810, Chicago, IL 60601. 13th & Joan books may be purchased for educational, business or sales promotional use. For information, please email the Sales Department at sales@13thandjoan.com.

Printed in the U. S. A.

First Printing, November 2020.

Library of Congress Cataloging-in-Publication Data has been applied for.

ISBN: 978-1-953156-26-6

DEDICATION

To Marie:
The love of my life. This is a gift from God, Jesus
and the Holy Spirit, of which I gift to you.
Thank you for always standing by my side.

"Natallanni's writing style is markedly transparent and reveals the powerful journey of discovery that frames his understanding of personality. One can find many points of connection as he shares profound personal stories and encourages self-reflection upon the different aspects of our own stories that shape us. I think this book is an excellent set-up for anyone who wants to do some inner work to determine their own motivations, heal from their hurts, and grow into greater awareness for better personal days ahead."

— Chris Lyons
Youth Pastor Bethany Community Church,
Seattle, Washington

"*Like. A. Phoenix.* provides much food for thought, both in looking at myself and in understanding other people in my life. Z.X.N's thoughts on the 'Outer Self' helped me to see my dad's life in a different light, allowing me to appreciate the good friend self he was to others, while accepting the father self that fell short of in my own hopes."

— Julie Reynolds,
Sr. Director
Close To My Heart

"When you pray for something... it can actually happen. And that is powerful!"

CHADWICK BOSEMAN

TABLE OF CONTENTS

FOREWORD

THE CONTENTS OF this book are the thoughts and researches of my mind and the times I've wondered about the inner workings of my inner self, or of my conscious-self. I believe that this book, if done correctly and read with an open mind, will change how we view our current placements in life as well as how we view our youth, our family lifestyles and our future. Life is an ever evolving roller coaster. There is no part of it that is predictable, no matter how things turn out. We as humans merely see selfishly ahead of us, and jealously behind us, it would be difficult for us not to. We will never know or come close to seeing the near death experiences, the woes that were moments away, the happiness that was just a single word or touch away, that we shut ourselves down from. As people, it is fair to say most of us travel to and from daily routines. During our journey, we pass by hundreds of faces, yet how many of those faces do we become familiar with? I tend to lean towards being optimistic. I yearn for friendship and closeness, yet I relish on the time spent alone to recoup. I adore the vast openness of conversing with intelligent and intellectual individuals who don't feed into bounderism, yet I still maintain walls to keep people at bay.

This book will aid in tearing down these walls. Together, I hope that you and I can explore a new theory. May we build a new structure, a new way to think, so to speak. We will transverse across the "ID," the consciousness, one's upbringing, religion, faith, community, and parenthood. I hope by the end of this book, you will have gained a clear understanding of who you really are; that you fully understand that you're kind, you are beautiful, you are wanted, you are needed, and most importantly, you are loved. At the end of the day, these things are what truly matters most. It is what our hearts should truly desire.

Take a walk with me...

CHAPTER 1
THE ONE SELF

'VE STARTED WRITING the beginning of this book over a dozen times. Not once did the different intros come out like the first one I wrote. I had to rewrite this because I was told diving into something that can be difficult in the beginning, it's not for everyone. You have to dip your toes in to see how warm the water is before you jump in to swim. So I started over, and over, and over. Not once did I like what I wrote. My decision was made and my foot was down and firmly placed. Start over...again. This would happen about ten, eleven, or twelve times. Then finally at 6:11am on a Saturday morning before heading out on a trip with my wife, the blank pages spoke to me. Before this had happened, I had already written most of the book, but I hadn't written things in a clear way. It was not clear because I didn't visualize what needed to be written. When I noticed this, it gave way to something new. The way a human brain is built and works is astonishing. What our minds are capable of achieving is remarkable. Did you know that you never actually forget anything you see and do in your life? Even the things you don't notice consciously, those things are recorded by the world's greatest camera. It is stored on the greatest, fastest and biggest server ever created. Your brain. Your problem isn't that you're too smart or not smart enough, it is not that you can't remember or have a terrible memory, it's that our ability to recall memories that makes us "weak" minded.

In my opinion everyone is born with the same amount of brain power or potential. The same strength. The same energy. It's how we harness and use said strength or energy that classifies and sets us apart. For a person to be able to access all of that energy and strength, depends on the amount of focus, motivation and dedication they put into the goals they're trying to accomplish. Hence the saying, "I've not reached my full potential." Have you ever heard of "The Mamba Mentality?" Pro basketball legend Kobe Bryant was known to have a great mentality and a gifted approach to greatness.

> *"The mindset isn't about seeking a result—it's more about the process of getting to that result. It's about the journey and the approach. It's a way of life. I do think that it's important, in all endeavors, to have that mentality."*
>
> — -Kobe Bryant,
> The Mamba Mentality: How I Play

Energy levels of the mind are very much different than that of the body. In fact the body is controlled by the mind. Picture your mind, and then look at a picture of the brain, and the nerve center. Now close your eyes and think of where you, your soul, call home in your body. Confused? I want you to try and pinpoint exactly where you are in your body. For me, it's my head. It's eye level. There is no above in my body's feeling, but there is definitely a below. If a doctor asks me where it hurts and I'm having chest pain, I've noticed my response is always "down here." If my stomach hurts I'm wondering, "what's going on down there?" But if it is pain or a headache, it feels close and magnified, like I'm being sandwiched in. I always say right here, in my head, is where it feels like home. For my friend John, it's his heart where he feels at home.

My wife however, is different. Her and I are polar opposites. My wife asks, "What do you mean by where you are in your body? I don't know how to answer that. I feel like I'm all of me and not just one part." I explained to her that thinking the way John and I do is not something that just happens. It develops over time as you allow your mind to be free and explore new areas of possibility. You may not think that way just yet. When you unlock different potentials in the mind, new ways of thinking and feeling will expand your views on experiences in life. This will help you understand one of the most important things you will ever ask yourself: "Who are you?" That will lead to hundreds or even thousands of other questions. The first of those being: where are you going and who do you want to be? It all begins with that first question. Who Are You?

Have you ever watched the show called *The Big Bang Theory*? This show happened to be a factor in who I am today and the catalyst for parts of this book. You see, my buddy is fascinated with physics and CERN's Large Hadron Collider located in Meyrin, Switzerland. The Collider is the center for the study of physics and all that is proven or disproven. I heard him talking about the show and decided to look into it, and what unfolded was a tremendous amount of self-discovery. Dealing with awkwardness and unsocialized people, these characters always have a YOU/WE factor that keeps them together no matter how awkward a person or moment was. You become who you hang out with the most. You will never know who you are for more than a few moments, due to our forever changing personalities. The key is to know who you are until you figure out who you want to be with, which is something some of us may never know. Still for others, we do, and it's who we surround ourselves with.

To be a healthy, balanced functioning person, one must have passion for what it is they want to do in life. What are you passionate about? Are you doing it now? Are you working towards conquering what makes you passionate? Does your passion drive you? I felt like I was surrounded by people who had passions and goals and were moving forward in life while I felt destined to fail. This was the source of the emptiness within me during a period in my life. Being passionless made me feel like I lacked emotion. It's like I was waiting for the next big thing to happen each day. If you feel like this, I have some advice for you. Quit waiting for the next best, big or exciting thing. Instead, have a reason to be excited in life right now.

When someone says, "everything happens for a reason" and you're going through a bad pattern, it's not that what you're going through is building for something better, but for a better you. A bad pattern can more than likely be from a poor choice or a series of poor choices that you have made and this is a repercussion of that. Learn from it. Build on it. Don't repeat the same mistakes. This is something I really needed to learn. I fail. I fall. That is human nature. The thing that makes me different is, I get up! Humans will make countless mistakes over a period of time. This will eventually cause us to fail and fall, but we must get up! Getting up is the key to overcoming failure. When we do fail, we must remember to not take anyone down with us, but to pick everyone up around us when we get up. This will help later on with not repeating the same mistakes. The times that I failed, I felt like my experiences and the things that I felt destroyed and numbed about didn't really affect me. I focused all my energy and mindset on the realization that if I fail, I have more opportunity to improve. I was now able to move on from things with an almost emotionless reaction to overcome the event of failing.

Let it be known, I was not suppressing my emotion. With risk comes an exceedingly high chance of failure. If you anticipate it, it is easier to accept and rebound from it than when you are ill-prepared for it. On occasion I may have felt like I was climbing up in life, I felt alone and vulnerable. There were points when I realized that I was higher up the ladder than I thought I could go. Knowing this made it harder to invest my full potential and focus on the task at hand. I've since learnt that many people feel this way. Only a few of those people know how to get beyond it in moments of despair. I'm going to share with you ways to overcome defeat and achieve your goals. What does it take to harness the mind's energy to focus on what's important?

Let's face it, not knowing what is meaningful to you, is what is part of the problem. Most of us have no focal point in our lives. Notice that I said "us." I too suffer from this "disorder," which was a source of emptiness within me. Growing up and even well into most of my adult life, I had no true close friends because of my unresolved emotional issues. Naturally, we try to fill this void with whatever feels right; but then we begin to notice afterwards that still, none of it feels right. So, ask yourself this: What is most important? Can you give an answer? I can. What is most important is you? Once you learn who you are and what you want, you understand that you are one of the most important aspects of your life. You just have to build from there. There is more to that and we will venture there soon.

CHAPTER 2
OPENING UP

I HAVE TO SAY, writing was no longer my strong suit. When I was a child, I wrote often and always had a book in my hands. Nowaday, I don't read as much as I used to and I'd become lazy at it. I would only read parts of things. Copy and paste was the only form of writing I did. What I didn't realize was that was also how I was living out my life. I was copying and pasting to mimic "friends" or to make new friends. I didn't really come into my own until I turned 30; and even then I was telling everyone I was 26 or 28. I did that because I felt I lost ten years of my life and I wanted them all back, but you cannot change time. I've learned that time is both your friend and your enemy. At certain points in your life, it may seem that time is all that you have, even though it's not. There is so much more to life than time, money, drugs, alcohol and partying. Most of my friends in their youth, spent all of their spare time preparing for a party-filled weekend. I was known for throwing wild parties and inviting hundreds of people. It was like it was a contest I was trying to win with myself. Truthfully, it was just that I was very alone and I wanted people to fill the void, but no matter what I did, no one filled it. The weird thing is, as soon as I was around people, I wanted them to leave. I enjoyed my alone time, and I was highly introverted, but forced myself to become a very strong extrovert through lots of training and practice. Unfortunately, it never helped. I always had the same feeling of loneliness. When I felt alone, I searched for ways to connect or reach for someone to love, even though the connection clearly was not there.

When I was 29 years old, I met this girl, we will call her Josie. Josie worked at the theme park that I frequented. In fact, my roommate was her boss. I told my roommate that I really liked this girl. My roommate was very clear, and said with the sternest face I'd ever seen,

"No, I forbid you to date that girl."

My roommate's boyfriend reiterated that same sentiment moments later. When I first met and said hello to Josie, it was the most awkward moment. I'm a hugger and Josie clearly was not. Still, she gave me a hug with a support beam notched in the ground between us. That, however, didn't faze me. She was an incredibly beautiful woman, on the outside. She was tall, with long blonde hair and a year-round bikini beach bod. This was perfect for her since we lived in Florida and going to the beach was a year-round option. Josie however, was extremely hurt and destroyed on the inside. She was in love with someone who'd never love her back and all of her attention and focus lived with him.

Eventually I'd get hired at the same place where Josie worked, and one day while completing orientation, I ran into Josie. Even in her uniform she turned heads. I approached her and said,

"Hey what's up..."I'd forgotten her name just that quick on the walk up! "Josie right?"

"Yes. Are you working here?"

"I do now. Just got hired. I'm going to be over at Spinnakers"

"That's cool. That's cool," as her voice trailed off leaving us in awkward silence, in a room filled with hundreds of people at that moment.

"So, what are you up to lately? I'd love to get together with you sometime and maybe hangout." I just wanted to get it over with and have the rejection done and move on.

"That would be great," she replied.

She gave me her number, much to my surprise.

"Okay I'll see you around," she said and scurried away to her table with her friends. It was like high school and I hated the feeling, but if it meant I had a shot with the prom queen, then it was worth it. In my head at that very moment, life was going to change and I was going to be a popular guy with the hot girlfriend, cool friends, and great job with lots of potential. For a while it looked like it was.

Boy was I dead wrong, but I wouldn't find that out until years later.

I never called Josie. In fact, I'd not think about her for months. I was preoccupied with work and finally getting ahead. After years of feeling like I was destined to fail, things were looking up in my life. But, like always, things took a turn and failure loomed, I got let go at work, and I was back to square one. Unhappy. I found a job at a sandwich shop, which was very close to the job I had before. I really loved the area because it gave me the feeling of being at home. My roommate and her boyfriend had decided to move out and I now lived alone. I was discouraged and a bit afraid of what would happen next in my life.

One day I was sitting at home watching TV, and a yellow piece of paper caught my eye. It was folded up as if a piece of gum was inside and tucked underneath the centerpiece on my table. I reached for it, and noticed Josie's handwriting. I put it down looking at it in dismay. I texted her. Ironically she'd just moved in across the road from me. She wasn't doing anything and wanted to meet up. I, being nervous of being alone with her, invited my friend Vince, to lighten up the mood. I went and picked her up and we went to the movies. It was February 8, 2008, and the latest movie release was *Fools Gold*. Josie, wasn't great when in big crowds, and the nerves of being on a first date, caused her to have a gigantic panic attic. The take-care-of-everything-and-everyone part of me quickly kicked in. We ended up leaving the theater right at the beginning of the film. I took Josie out to eat, and we talked and laughed all night. Things went great. I dropped her off and figured I may have a shot at making a relationship work and getting a taste of love. I texted her later in the week, and I got no response. It turns out her friend knew someone that had the same name as me and that friend was a total cheat and loser. Josie got the two of us mixed up. She came over with her friend to grab some things she'd left in my car, and her friend saw me and told Josie that I wasn't the guy she was thinking of. Josie later texted me about the situation and we decided to hang out again. On Valentine's Day that year, I went out and purchased an obnoxiously large card and roses. We were meeting friends in Daytona Beach for some karaoke and to watch a band play. The date went great. I liked her and told her we should be together.

She said, "You don't want to date me."

I responded with, "Sure I do. Why wouldn't I?"

"Well because, I'm not the dateable type. I'm broken," she said.

In hindsight, that should've been the first red flag. I was not ready to lead anyone and should've been mature enough to know that. But I quickly responded with, "Well that's perfect, I like to fix broken things."

She laughed, and we danced. She would go home and leave me waiting for that first kiss. For six more days. I invited her over to experience the full lunar eclipse. My apartment was facing the opposite direction, but if you leaned over the balcony you could see it. She loved it. I would not take a glimpse at the eclipse the whole night, because everything I wanted to see at that precise moment was standing right in front of me on my balcony. She came back to the couch on my balcony and cuddled with me. Holding this woman felt like I had the whole world in my hands. She would later ask me where my bathroom was. Even though there were two and one was closer, I directed her to the one in my room. She went in. I wanted her to. My room was super tidy and neat and I wanted her to notice it. Because I felt like it made me more of a normal person and made me more desirable.. When she re-emerged from the bathroom, we sat together again on my balcony. There were people inside playing rock band, but none of that mattered. All of my attention was on Josie and the moment that was about to happen next. I took a tiny box out of my pocket and handed it to her.

"What's this?" she asked

"My mom told me that if I met a woman that I like, if she was different, I had to do something that sets me apart from anyone else that may be courting her. She said I need-ed to make her remember me."

"And so you're giving me this box?" she asked.

"Open it!" I said excitedly.

She did. It was a necklace I'd seen and wanted her to have. She loved it. I asked her out that night and she said yes. I got the kiss and she got a cuddle buddy on a couch while a full eclipse was taking place. All seemed to be right at that moment.

Wrong.

Like you who are reading this, I got caught up in the beautiful moment, I didn't see the signs and warnings that could've helped Josie and I's relationship. Key points that would later destroy my love for her, and her love for me. I searched for reasons to find connections where I should have never looked. Because these were false teachings. I had to come to an understanding. I don't think Josie and I were meant to be together. She was meant to get me to move across the country, not meant to stay in my life. You see, Josie was a leaf. As were many people I'd later encounter in my life. Josie was not a branch. I tried to make her into one. That was a terrible mistake I'd make in an attempt to bring stability into my life and it would instead start to rot my tree. You see, your life is a tree. Your upbringing and your childhood are the roots and nutrients. The trunk of the tree is your adulthood, the branches are the family and lifelong friends you naturally make along the way. Occasionally, you'll meet leaves, or people, that will open doorways to new branches and seeds for new trees. They are there for a season, and meant to move on. When you try to keep a leaf, it drains all the energy and life from your branches. It becomes a cancer. You must learn to let it go. It may return as a new leaf, or become a branch. Only time will tell.

Josie and I's relationship started just before the recession began. She would move to the west coast and settle in California with her parents to help them out. I would follow West, but I moved to Seattle. I worked hard and asked her to move up once I was settled and she agreed to come. A few days before she came, she called like she always did. It was snowing, which I'd never seen before. I'd seen snow, but not while it fell. It was beautiful, and I was in a happy place. I had just finished closing up the store where I worked and was taking out the trash. She stopped me from describing how I was feeling at that moment to say,

"I don't think we should be together anymore."

"What? Why? What are you saying?"

"I'm saying that we don't work. I'm saying you're not my preference."

"Preference? What the heck do you mean by preference?"

Be careful what you ask for. What she replied with started me down a road of hatred and depression that would last for close to six months.

"I can't date you anymore, because you're Black. I don't like Black men."

I hung up.

She still moved up. We became roommates and our friendship, or what was left of it, dissolved daily. Any emotional turmoil she had, was used on me. One day, I was at a local coffee house I frequented. I was with a friend from overseas. I got a phone call from Josie. She had not received her tuition check and hadn't been able to find a job. She was going to be late on rent and didn't have a time frame of when she could pay. She had refused my help before, and now she needed it. I don't remember exactly what she said that caused me to say the words I would say to her, but whatever it was, six months of emotional frustration and resentment came out in one sentence. I said,

"Josie, I love you. I really do. But you're by far the worst thing that has ever happened to me."

That was the very worst thing I've ever said to anyone. It hurt her. It bothered me for years.

Josie gasped, hung up and packed her entire life up and left. She erased herself from my life in less than two hours. I saw her once more after that, and then never again.

Josie, if you're reading this, I'm truly and deeply sorry. You deserved better. You deserved more. You deserved release and a better life. You helped me in so many ways. In ways you'll never know. I owe you an apology and I'm sending it to you the only way I can, this way. I also forgive you. For everything we went through both my fault and yours. It was both of our faults. I wish and pray for the best for you and your husband. You deserve happiness.

Those first six months in Seattle ended up being the catalyst to a better life for me. I lost the most important woman I'd ever known, my mom, during that stretch, I met my best friend Laura, and the long journey of reconstructing my life started. It would begin in a parking lot on my birthday with a new girlfriend that handed me one of the most symbolic gifts I've ever received in my life to this day. She handed me an eraser, and told me my past was my past, I can erase the bad parts by making new good parts. I didn't have to live the life that was destroying me.

Thus began my transition of burning and burying my past. From within the ashes a phoenix was born. The phoenix, though mythical, is metaphorically my spirit animal. I believe that everyone goes through a burnout and is reborn in new ways. For some more often than others. What does a rebirth look like? It looks a lot like a mess at first, but if worked out, both rebirth, and life becomes a beautiful thing. It becomes a rebirth of you and your emotional and spiritual journey. Your life should be full of color, love, respect and balance. Let me show you how to get there. Picture yourself standing on a hillside, and your life is laid out before you. All your accomplishments, disappointments, your relationships and your friendships. Now imagine you've been depressed for all of it. Rather than seeing this prolific colorful spectacle of life, you see shades of black and gray and some white. Off in the distance, you see a small flower. The flower is weak, but brightly colored in orange. The more you focus on this flower, the brighter and stronger it gets. That is how you have to view hope. Happiness. It is the color you will add to your life. As you let this hope and wonder build inside you, the flower blooms, letting it's color spill all over and run deep into the valley that is your life. Your life gives way to the most amazing colors and views beyond your imagination.

Then comes the self-realization that you have finally found the most important thing. You. The first thing to know when you've found yourself is this: you're not the center of it all. Those you love and have around you will be the center, but they will help you understand and appreciate your life. I've seen it. It happens, it is true. It takes work. Happiness is not a place you can arrive at. It is a state you can cultivate. Develop and grow. Like. A. Phoenix.

CHAPTER 3
THE INTRODUCTION OF THE ONE SELF

W E ALL HAVE moments in our lives when it seems that things happen for no apparent reason. There will be times when we lose all that matters to us at the last moment before success is clutched in our hands. We know there are some moments that could be better, leaving us with a distinct feeling of loneliness and being dispensable. We all go through moments where things are simply, at their worst. But it is then, that we activate or acknowledge the inner workings of our true self. Whether that's rooted in hatred, selfishness, aggression, or love, selflessness and hope. Either way we tend to use the inner workings of ourselves to either enrich or torment our lives. Some of us however, are deceived. Life can be distorted and our decisions can be swayed by money, greed, and chaos. Unfortunately, those things can easily replace reason, companionship and love. We can easily be, and are often, influenced by social media, news, music, and television.

However, there is hope. I believe that hope is something created by God and instilled in us all for times of darkness, dishonesty and loneliness. We are all connected. All of our paths somehow connect in ways we may never fully understand. We may never know it. We may never feel it. I tell you though, the connection is there. We move and venture out into our daily lives based on decisions that are influenced by our surroundings on a daily basis. These decisions are usually either based on selfishness or selflessness. Both of these two words are an extension of "the inner self." However, there is another way to describe this extension. It is a word relatively used more often than one may think. That word is -ish. You are about to see how these three letters together can change the way you will think about the daily decisions you make regarding your inner self. Oh wait, I seemed to have gotten ahead of myself. You see I've forgotten to tell you what ish is, silly me, I guess I am rather tired...ish. See what I did there?

Ish is an adverb that can be defined as: to some extent. It is a very small piece to a rather complex theory (Oxford Language). You see ish is that indecision you have when you can't make up your mind about what food you want to eat for a meal, what dress you want to wear for a party, what song you need to hear to make you forget, or bring you back. That tiny bit of doubt you have when you realize that maybe this is the wrong time or the wrong decision. In that tiny half millisecond, that tiny bit of questioning can either bring worlds crashing down or build entirely

24

new ones. It can close doors or open up many more. Ah yes, the door, a pathway to something more daunting than what preceded it, or a road to an incredible new experience. This, ladies and gentlemen, is where we encounter our first exploration into a new way of thinking.

In 1923, Sigmund Freud, renowned for being the founder and father of psychoanalysis, wrote *The Ego and The Id,* a predecessor to his collection of theories on the conscious, the unconscious and the preconscious. These writings were based on the daily lives of those who lived during his time. The id, ego, and superego are Freud's explanations of three distinct, yet interacting agents. Freud's structural model of the psyche talks about three theoretical terms whose activity and interaction of our mental state determine and describe our mental life. Freud suggests that the id is the set of uncoordinated instinct trends, the super-ego plays the critical and moralizing roles, and the ego is the organized and realistic part that mediates between the desires of the id and the super-ego.

> *"The functional importance of the ego is manifested in the fact that normal control over the approaches to motility devolves upon it. Thus in its relation to the id it is like a man on horseback, who has to hold in check the superior strength of the horse; with this difference, that the rider tries to do so with his own strength while the ego uses borrowed forces. The analogy may be*

carried a little further. Often a rider, if he is not to be parted from his horse, is obliged to guide it where it wants to go; so in the same way the ego is in the habit of transforming the id's will into action as if it were its own."

— *Sigmund Freud*

Over the course of the 97 years since Freud's writings were published, our world has changed dramatically. Social status has never been more evident than it is today. Your status can be influenced by television, Hollywood, social media and journalistic views of what is the norm or what the next big thing will be. I believe that theory should change and evolve or become new just as time changes. Theory can be defined as: a supposition or a system of ideas intended to explain something, especially one based on general principles independent of the thing being explained (Oxford Language). My theory henceforth can be known as Natallanni's Theory of The One Self. The *One Self* can be defined as: the human personality broken down into four conceptual versions called core parts of consciousness (Like. A. Phoenix).

Everyone is born with the same basic personality that is split into four parts. These four parts are then built on with outliers, which allows a person to ultimately become their true self. That can take about 30 years for the general population to achieve. The one self is your everyday self and consists of these four parts:

THE INNER SELF: This is the process of seeing yourself as you really are. It is the personality stripped down of all ego and false confidence, leaving an unembellished profile of one's true identity. More precisely put, everything that makes the inner self is what truly lies in the deepest depths of your mind and soul. It is the unconditional, yet pertinent, you. *Example*: What you do, say or think when no one will have knowledge of the outcome, is who you truly are, or what you truly want or perceive yourself to be. Worldly views, people, materialistic items or loved ones, do not tend to influence these values. It is where morals live and are formed and where true love exists for those who are at peace and balanced.

THE OUTER SELF: This is the you that you allow the world to see you as. It is dictated or influenced by the world around you. The outer self is the first part of you that comes in multiple versions. This is not bi-polarism or split personalities. This multi-you is a true form of yourself. *Example*: You are one type of yourself when you are around your mother, while another form of yourself at work or at school. Additionally you are a different version of yourself in front of friends and yet still another version with a significant other. Each part seems like one and the same, but you can never share the same parts of you over and over with multiple people because there are many factors into what makes what version of yourself relevant in each moment. Like environment, relationship, history, mood etc. *Example*: Your Instagram or Facebook posts that show the best version of yourself is your outer self. The information you let your family or co-workers learn about you is your outer self.

THE ADVERSE SELF: this is everything that you are not. It creates a false you and temporarily flashes itself at the most inopportune time. The adverse self is who a person wants to be. Smart, good looks, has all the answers and can accomplish anything. Nothing is too hard or too weird. This is the invincible part of One Self, the "nothing can go bad, and I'll be cool or seen as a legend" self. This is where reality separates from illusion. This version of one self derives from the social norms of the society surrounding you, by becoming easily influenced by social media, your inner circle, Hollywood and journalism. The adverse self is the brain-washed, inauthentic or subversion of you that you think you are. It is the epitome of false confidence or being egotistical, but can change at a moment's notice because it is influenced by the hierarchy of a social status.

THE APPOSITE SELF: This is the inner, outer and adverse selves struggling with each other within our daily lives. It is the difference between what is right and what is wrong. The Apposite Self identifies what you value and stand for, but predicates itself by announcing the other side of the way you think. It shows you the "what if's" and the "what not's," if you would choose to approach your current situation from a different perspective. *Example*: You should be home studying for your final, but you choose to go out and party because everyone is doing it and this party will help you relieve the stress of studying. Or another *example*: You take a call from an ex-boyfriend or ex-girlfriend, and you know you shouldn't go out with them and get back into the chaotic mess you were in, but you miss them and place yourself in an unhealthy situation. The Apposite Self is where thoughts are formed and where decisions are made. It is also where depression comes to light. More on that later.

Each person has a unique personality made up of these four core parts. Depending on a particular surrounding, upbringing, culture, or geographical location, one can have a certain part or parts of the One Self stronger than the others, while others have the four core parts constantly battling for dominance. A healthy One Self has all four parts working simultaneously and congruently together at all times. One of the four will take over depending on the situation to be dealt with. Let's dive in this a little bit more in the next chapter.

CHAPTER 4

THE CRISIS OF AN UNBALANCED ONE SELF

I SAID IN THE beginning that you don't know who you are until you become who you are. And for some of us, we may never know. Still for others, we do, and it's who we surround ourselves with. We are going to jump right in and unpack my takings on the *One Self*. Like with time or technology, the inner workings of the *One Self* changes and updates on a daily basis. Sigmund Fraud's research and findings don't mean the same today as they did in the early 1900s. In today's society, we have a lot of distractions and things available to us at a much faster speed. It sometimes feels as if instantaneous is not fast enough. Like the world went out and got itself into a big rush for nothing. One can sit at home and purchase everything from a car or a home to clothes and food. They can watch a film, and even meet the person they choose to marry, all from the comforts of their home. If times have changed the way we think, then why have we not changed how we think about the times and where we've come from?

We tend to look at growth, albeit a youthful mistake, as an instant and continual pattern that shows immediate change. This is not always the case. Picture growth as a garden. You plant seeds, water them and then you have to thin those out to allow for ambient nutrition. Growth takes time. And you won't know how good that growth can be until the seeds have harvested. Change can be viewed in this same manner. Growth in economic thresholds of the world can signify either the start or end to certain parties of people in governments, classes of people, communities or even entire populations. History has proven that not all growth is or can be good. Metropolitan growth spurts can lead to destruction of green ways, forestry, loss of plant and animal life, and of course gentrification. Gentrification is a new term defined as: The process of renovating and improving a house or district so that it conforms to middle-class taste. To do this, the lower class, must be forced to either become a part of the middle class, or move to another affordable area. (Oxford Languages) Let's take this term and apply this to everyday day life as we focus on the inner self.

I'm going to explore with you my findings, regarding what we go through now, and how it differs from 97 years ago. I want you to get out three glasses or cups. I'd like you to place them on the table in a line so that all three glasses are visible to you. Leaving the glass in the middle, I want you to fill the other two with ¾ of water and return them to their proper places on the table. Now get a piece of scratch paper. Tear this paper into three even pieces, making sure that they're big enough to write on. On one paper write: *My Parents and Family*. On the next write: *Me*. On the last paper write: *My Community*. Place these in front of each glass left to right.

Most parents raised their children with the best intentions. They made choices based on what they thought was best for your future. For the majority of you who have chosen to read this book, the above statement may be truthful. See, your parents raised you through three different lenses: the world surrounding you, how they were raised, and what financial state they were in at the time of your birth. These three things were the basis of what you were to become. Your community is the other major influencer in your upbringing. If you live in a rural neighborhood with no crime and good schools with a middle class family, life may have been great and you grew up feeling like you're able to conquer the world on your own based off on what the community has shown and taught you, as well as your parents' teachings.

If each of these pitchers, the parents, and the community, are pouring water into the middle glass at the same time, you'll notice that everything mixes in nicely and the glass in the middle becomes full. The middle glass, which is you, may be fully content with where life is at the moment. You are ready to embrace change, opportunity and to be an adult. However based on my findings, I believe that you are actually at least twelve to thirteen years away from accomplishing this. Picture yourself at age eighteen. You may have seen yourself as confident, intelligent, and ready to conquer the world. For a majority of us, we were in fact very vulnerable and highly inexperienced at life. We were naïve to think otherwise. What I mean is this, EVERYONE has a moment of severe traumatization. Either it happens to you, the individual, or someone very close to you, or you witness something horrific and life halts itself and everything you've ever learned drops into one single worded question: Why? My father once told me that that single three-lettered word is the only question that can never be answered. It drives children to learn about the world around them. It leads researchers and scientists to new and unexplored discoveries. "Why" can change the course of a person's entire life. When one experiences trauma, they inexplicably hit the reset button. They question everything they have ever valued and learned and either one of two things can happen. That person will adapt to change and "grow up" or they never learn from what they have just experienced and will continue down a path that will lead them to an eventual mid-life crisis. There are seven stages our personalities go through throughout our lives. Let's pinpoint those here and then talk about what it looks like when we skip one of these stages.

APPROPRIATING: As a new born we are utterly defenseless from 0–8 years of age. We are respectfully parasitic as we rely totally on our parents for survival. Parents will give parts of themselves willingly to support the growth of their child. However, there are parts of the parents' personalities that children will learn and take from without the parents knowing. An example would be the way a parent speaks on the phone versus how a friend or relative speaks on the phone, and how that we, as children, will mimic that in our own everyday life. This action is generally shown in playtime. At this stage we are borrowing mannerisms and actions from the adults in our lives, and using those things to develop our personality in order to find out who we are and what we want to be.

ATTAINING: The 9–17 years stage can be described as the "coming of age" point in life. We learn a lot about who we are as an individual and we start to break away from borrowed mannerisms and begin to form our own. Decision making becomes a desire. It's a grown up thing to do and we aspire to be an equal by being allowed to make decisions in our day to day lives. This stage is also where we figure out a lot about our bodies and it's a frightening experience for most, because we don't fully understand or contemplate the changes taking place. Through experiencing puberty, we learn about who we want to be around and start to figure out who we are. We learn from this by surrounding ourselves with someone who is experiencing the same symptoms we are currently experiencing or by finding someone who just understands what we are experiencing. We start to really develop the four core parts of our personality, which are the Inner, Outer, Adverse and Apposite Selves.

NASCENT: This stage is when 18-22 year-olds really start to come into existence and self-reliance is prevalent throughout our personality and daily life. It is here that we will question everything we've learned and absorbed in our young lives. The majority of us will experience a traumatic event of some sort in our lives or experience it through someone around us. This is where we must hit the reset button and question everything we know and value. This is not a bad thing to do. Once we have questioned all that we have learned, and then we replace what information we don't connect with, we tend to adopt new information, morals and beliefs as our own. To process this reset we will dump all we've obtained and reload it with the same, or new information. For those of us that decided not to process, but move on from the event, we will be left with a misguided and upside down placement later in life, which is called a mid-life crisis.

REFORM: The reform stage is where we as 23-29 year olds truly turn into ourselves. Like taste buds, our personalities will change every four to eight years, as we adapt to life and our surroundings. This age group will mature best when the quality of their surroundings and the time spent exploring life, and filling it with fun and meaningful relationships are made a top priority. The reform period is a transition into true adulthood. This stage is the last years of individualism of the young adult life and for those of us that do not have the opportunity to fully transition into the next stage before kids and marriage, they tend to feel trapped and need to get away more often than not. This is a very important time for growth, as we move past thinking about ourselves and our own unique goals, to thinking for our future and preparing for a partner that will be around us forever. Most who are in this stage will reform their job, diets, habits and relationships (this includes friendships, family and romantic partners), to be equal to the goals that are going to make up their life for the foreseeable future.

SUPERLATIVE: The Superlative era is one of completeness. There is a belief that the twenties are the best years of one's life, but that is not true. Remember when I told you that you were at least twelve to thirteen years away from accomplishing maturity as an adult? Well, here's why. Years 30-59 are the years of contentment. Those who find themselves here are content with life and all that it offers, where life is going and the future at hand. Not many changes are made that are not already planned or in motion. The superlative period is the first stage that is longer than nine years. These are the years a person will tend to focus on the sustainability of their environment as well as the health and financial placements of their family. Those in this stage learn to plan for death and the future of their family. In turn, we will discover our purpose in life, some will be able to achieve this, whilst others will not. Caring for others, i.e. children, parents, lovers or friends, will become a vital piece of this period. This action will be of significant importance as we approach the next stage.

GOLDEN ERA: Years 60-79 are considered the golden years of life. People here tend to retire and travel the world. During the golden era, people will start to scratch off things from their bucket list they've created during the first 60 years of life. Let's not get confused and see this as a crisis. This is not a now-or-never push either. The golden years is a rebirth of youthfulness as we head into the final stages of life. One thing to be learned about this stage is that we are no longer afraid of death, because we know it is now closer than it has ever been before. We will instead accept not only that death is coming but also that it is inevitable and we will start to walk *with* death, by being prepared for it with all we do. When we travel, make financial plans, or help family out, we will do so by making sure that we are prepared for death like it was expected and not leave unfinished business behind for our families to cope with. Small things that were once taken for granted in the past, will now mean more, whilst materialistic things tend to take a back seat in life, as we learn that we will leave this life as we've entered it. With nothing.

TWILIGHT ERA: Years 80-End of life. The significance of this period is that death is now inevitable. Most who are lucky to have reached this stage, realize this and now await it willingly. The common concept is that this life cannot be over when we take that final breath, but rather we embrace it knowing fully, that there is another stage of life after this one. We make sure that we do all that we are meant to do on this earth. All that is good will be of importance and building our family for a better future and legacy becomes the goal. We will leave lasting marks in order to make sure the proper goals and practices are followed long after we are gone. For many, memories of our existence will fade within one to two generations, but for a select few, a lasting mark will be indented into the family legacy for generations to come.

CHAPTER 5

THE CLUTTER OF THE MID LIFE CRISIS

WE DEFINE A *Mid-Life Crisis* as: an emotional crisis of identity or self-confidence that can occur in early middle age adults. Although age is not an accurate or sole indicator in determining if someone is going through a midlife crisis, there are some sure signs a person is moving through one, such as, buying an expensive sports car or jewelry, or getting younger friends/lovers, or hanging out at college parties, or siphoning off savings and other accounts. A midlife crisis can happen to any man or woman, and can often strike between the ages of 35 and 55. While this is a painful process for the person experiencing the crisis, it is also painful for the people involved in that person's life. A majority of men experiencing a midlife crisis will focus on their achievement and the desire to prove their success. With women however, it can be a fixation on their physical appearance, sexual attraction, and what's next after parenthood. In a study called "Midlife In The United States" or MIDUS, researchers have shown that only about 10-20% of the U.S. population has a legitimate, identifiable midlife crisis. A few of those who are experiencing a midlife crisis, manage to work their way through the crisis without too much trouble, but others struggle to find balance in their life again. The process of growing up and undergoing maturation signifies the passing of one's youth. There are millions of people struggling with these feelings on a daily basis.

So what is a midlife crisis? It was a term created by Elliot Jacques in 1965. It was widely used by Freudian psychologists. Back then it was described as a normal period during the lifespan, when we transition from young people to older adults. During this time, adults evaluate their achievements, goals, and dreams against what they had wished for in the past, and what stage they are facing in life. However I believe a midlife crisis is a rebirth of a traumatic experience that was not dealt with while experiencing it. This individual did not reset and think about what they've learned, nor did they choose to question the information placed before them. They've just been on auto pilot and all the information put in was never processed, broken down and determined how it impacted who they were. It becomes a cluttered mess. The four core parts have no clear distinction of what part is in control signifying the activation of *The Adverse Self* and this results in the reset to where things were working perfectly. That could be college, high school, pre-marriage, the honeymoon years or whatever that person feels is appropriate. Now they have to determine what they want and figure out how to get it. If they determine that it is goals and achievements, the pain is less experienced. If it is just a fear of missing out or the lack of wanting to grow old, well then the outcome is inevitable. Take me for example. I'm a forty year old man who, for the first time, feels like I'm accomplishing goals. I experienced many formidable events in my life and only recently (five years ago) started to process and learn from them. This made me a better person, but showed me that I was not good at any one thing in my life, further making me realize how much of a failure I was, and how much I relied on everyone and everything around me to survive. I had become exactly what I feared, a living parasite. I had so much talent, but I could never just focus on one project. I instead tried to do it all and prove all my doubters wrong, thus my efforts resulted in no achievements and nobody I could call when I was in need of any assistance. I merely succeeded at proving myself wrong and everyone else right. This both bothered and puzzled me. I sunk into work mode, started dating women a few years too young for me, and lived in a college neighborhood. So I asked those around me and researched my approach towards life. I changed my life by figuring out who I was, and where I had come from and slowly started to take focus on self-love. I met an incredibly beautiful and amazing woman and eventually we got married. I have a career with amazing benefits and co-workers. I have lifelong friendships with people that I trust and who trust me. I no longer seek out the gratification of others but rather my own heart felt acceptance. Only recently have I begun to notice how much my peers and I have grown over the years. In fact, just yesterday, a friend called me and while inquiring about this very book you're reading, said that she felt that I'm just now getting started with adulthood. I had not mentioned to her that I was writing about this. I did agree with what she said. I created a term for this. I'm what I refer to as a "Late Bloomer."

I define Late Bloomer as: A person or persons experiencing a delayed or late coming of adulthood maturation. An example is someone that does not come into his or her own, either mentally or physically, until after most of their peers have matured. Another example is a person whose talents or capabilities are not visible to others until later than usual, someone who becomes successful, attractive, or mentally stable at a later time in life than most people develop. Late-Bloomers tend to relish on the new found discovery of their capability, and use it to better those around them. It becomes an instrument of wisdom, rather than one of personal gain. This is only true if maturation is in place.

Maturation or **Maturing** can be explained not only by the physical growth of one's body but also by the growth of the mind or One Self and the personalities within the One Self. What I believe is this: the four core parts of the One Self are four personalities of an individual. I find that these four parts are a continual jubilation of collaborative work from the time a person matures to the day we stop function-ing as a person in our society. To mature, the One Self must develop. To be fully developed, the four core parts need to be self-functioning, and work together seamlessly. When all four parts of the One Self work together congruently, this is our daily routine. *Example*: we start our day with just our inner self. This is when we wake up and prepare our minds for the day ahead. That can be done by lying in bed and meditating, catching up on processing yester-day's interactions, or preparing your mind for the day that lies ahead. Our outer self kicks in when we decide what clothes we will wear, what food we will eat at work, how we choose to answer certain emails, and then proceed into the morning communications of social media, text messag-es etc. The Adverse self is the smallest part of the four, for most people. It is the angry response to problems that you want to show like quitting, walking out, or even giving up. It's everything that you are not, but you're making yourself seem like you are. It is also when a person wants to show off to impress someone with something. The adverse self symbolizes the exact opposite of what a person wants. Now let me hit on that just a bit more. If you want something, it is either because you need it or simply because you desire it. A *desire* is something you can completely function without, like luxury cars, a model girlfriend/boyfriend, an active nightlife, a yacht, etc. A *need* is a roof over your head, a working vehicle, a good steady and healthy job, consistent healthy meals, family, friends, love, God. It is human nature to send and receive information and we tend to send signals of what we desire more often than any other signals. The apposite-self kicks in when we are on our way to work and someone is trying to cut into your lane while in traffic, do you let them in or not? When we get to work, do we hold the door or the elevator for the person behind or not? Do you decide to talk to the stranger on a train, plane or bus? The Apposite self is where decisions are made. I believe this is where indecisiveness is developed and confusion/unhappiness starts. Our inner most desires are born here and so this is a perfect place to create the environment needed for depression. The chart below will explain the cons of an unhealthy unbalanced One Self.

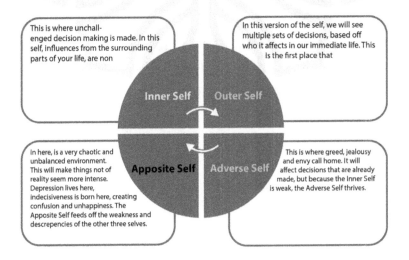

This is where unchall-enged decision making is made. In this self, influences from the surrounding parts of your life, are non

In this version of the self, we will see multiple sets of decisions, based off who it affects in our immediate life. This is the first place that

Inner Self   **Outer Self**

Apposite Self   **Adverse Self**

In here, is a very chaotic and unbalanced environment. This will make things not of reality seem more intense. Depression lives here, indecisiveness is born here, creating confusion and unhappiness. The Apposite Self feeds off the weakness and descrepencies of the other three selves.

This is where greed, jealousy and envy call home. It will affect decisions that are already made, but because the Inner Self is weak, the Adverse Self thrives.

In this Healthy vs. Unhealthy chart, you will notice that all the blue blocks of the Healthy One Self are leveled in all four selves. This would indicate a working One Self that has a healthy balanced lifestyle. In the Semi-Healthy blocks that are red, you see slightly skewed variances between the four blocks. While not healthy, there are small changes that can be made to correct what is wrong in order to live a better life. However in the green blocks, we see something totally different. We first notice the elephant in the room, which is that the Apposite self is by far bigger than that of the other four. You see, when unbalanced, something different happens if the Apposite self takes charge. Apposite is defined as: apt in the circumstances or in relation to something (Oxford Language). When opposites struggle against one another, this is when the Apposite takes charge. It is because the other three are in constant struggle for power.

It's power is x3 due to taking on all three core selves and making it into one. This is why depression is so huge and seems like a massive mountain to climb.

CHAPTER 6

THE FIRST KEY TO HAPPINESS

THE KEY TO finding ourselves and finding out who we are and who we aspire to be, is to know that a balanced life, while it starts with us, is not about us. It's about the people around us, the creatures, environments and relationships we build and interact with. That is what life is about. If it was just about us, we'd have no need or desire to spread out and explore or get involved in seeking love and companionship. If there is one piece of advice that is useful to everyone on Earth and universally applicable, it is that balance is the key to everything.

Balance is defined as: an even distribution of weight enabling someone or something to remain upright and steady; harmonious of design and proportion (Oxford Language). True balance of any one thing means that one item or items will have freedom of movement. These items can then sway in a direction with the changes in the conditions of the environment of which it will face. But no matter what the item faces, it will not bend, break or fall. It will withstand the test of which it is receiving and withstand the forces of nature. The same can be said in life. You don't give in or let go of what is true to you. Balance does not mean perfection. Life is meant to be shaken, it keeps one humble and on their toes. Why is that? Well for starters there are many variables that are involved in living day to day. We are surrounded by and often dependent on many people, things, formats and structures in order for us to function. That is the way our society has conformed during our time and generation. These variables influence our decision making, actions and interactions with one another. I've constructed a graph that will help you understand how to balance life and these variables. It will be followed by concise explanations for each step of the graph.

Natallanni's Relative Pyramid to One-Self

Healthy Balanced Work Life

Supportive Positive Community

Healthy Friendships/Relationships

Functional Home/Environment

Consistent Exercise

Healthy Food

Mental Recharge

Sleep (6 Hours)

Balance

One Self

ONE-SELF: The Pyramid has One-Self at the bottom. This is one of the first keys to balance, and therefore it is extremely important. When you know who you are, and where you want to go, a plan can be made. When a plan is made, system can be followed and a balance is formed at the base.

BALANCE: To achieve balance, you must first learn it. You must learn to say no, just as you have learned to say yes. You have to know when to move on and understand the difference between moving on, and quitting and giving up. You must always work hard, but never stretch yourself too thin. Moderation is a key component as well.

Moderation = Balance. Balance = Moderation.

SLEEP: This is another key factor in the health of the One Self. Six hours of sleep is the minimum amount needed to make healthy decisions, to have healthy thoughts, and to function with a proper mind. Like your body, your mind and consciousness need a break too. Slowing down and allowing your brain and spirit to rest is a vital piece of becoming a more rounded and complete person.

MENTAL RECHARGE: I don't know about you, but when I was younger I never had moments dedicated to myself. This would eventually dampen my mood to be around people. I became bitter about who I was with and where I was. Once

I started giving myself room to be alone and recharge, I became a more constructive and positive person to be around.

CONSISTENT EXERCISE: For some of you, this will be the hardest one of all to accomplish. Every time you can, you may use an excuse not to exercise, but you must not do that. Get up, run, walk fast, bike, play, run to grab a coffee at the coffeehouse, as long as you start to be active. Being active changed my life and has helped transform me into a better person. Exercising on a regular basis is a needed asset to becoming a more complete person.

FUNCTIONAL HOME & ENVIRONMENT: I cannot stress enough how important it is that your home and living environment be of sound and peaceful harmony. Many of us have at some point lived in an unhealthy environment. It does not allow for growth, love, humility, or learning. Each of which are food for the soul.

HEALTHY FRIENDSHIPS & RELATIONSHIPS: You may have heard the expression you get out of life what you put in life. Relationships are some of the most important decisions you may ever make in your life. They literally have the power to make or break a person's life. Worse, it can destroy or end a life, should we choose to interact with the wrong individual. Happiness is not a thing that is brought on by temporary fixation or relationship. Learn to distinguish between what is temporary and what is a life defining friendship.

SUPPORTIVE POSITIVE COMMUNITY: Like your home, having a very supportive and positive community is very vital to the development of the One Self. You are a sponge. Your brain is constantly learning new ways to communicate and interact with the environment around you. Make it easy on yourself and be sure to surround yourself with the right people in the right environment.

HEALTHY BALANCED WORK LIFE: You will spend more time with the people you work with than your own family. Everyday millions of people get up and head to jobs they don't like. Most don't realize that they are commiting spiritual suicide. You will kill yourself by going to a job that destroys you piece by piece day by day. Seek the job that drives you and makes you happy. Let it not just support you financially, but be a part of your positive community. You need to seek support emotionally, and if possible, spiritually. Your job can be one that with each advancement, symbolizes a rebirth of growth in you. Like. A. Phoenix.

CHAPTER 7
OWNING UP TO LEVEL UP.

THIS IS ANOTHER pivotal resource in finding our One Self. As a society here in America, we've learned to point fingers and do anything we can to avoid the truth. The truth of which is that: we must work for excellence, step up to challenges, take ownership of our mistakes and always move forward. This is the recipe for being a champion. After the Great Depression, generations that lived through that time realized they were not as prepared as they thought they were. Many went out and started working hard. They had their head down, mouth closed, and eyes open. They were able to provide a stable home and a safety plan for their families and their future. At some point, that changed drastically. Research can show technology is to blame for that. The advancement of technology should lead to advancement of the mind. Advancement of the mind should lead to advancement of humankind.

Technology is to blame for the change of people working hard. Rather than technology making things easier for people to place more focus on achieving goals and gaining more education, it is argued that technology has driven humanity into a state of laziness and reliability. This also has placed our generations into a world of "instantaneousness," but the advancement of the technology should lead to the advancement of the mind. Advancement of the mind should lead to advancement of the human-race, which should lead to the advancement of life itself. It should all balance out in the end, leaving nothing behind. However, it doesn't balance out. Instead we tend to look for the easy way out. Theft, schemes and bribery, now replace ingenuity, creativity and continuity.

Life mistakes are another part of this equation. Taking risks and failing, or just poor decision makings can have lasting effects on one life and the future of those involved and invested in a person. I believe that within the last few decades, people have begun to worry that if they actually owned up to their mistakes, they'd risk not going anywhere in life. So the blame game started. "I lived in this kind of household, or my family was this." And then like most things, that started to develop overtime we entered suing for capital gains and pointing fingers at governments, because nothing is as it seems and everything is terrible right now. Well no, it's not. Everything is amazing right now and we are whining simply because we know we now have no choice but to work and to fix the problems our society's lifestyle has created. If we don't bridge the gap between so-cial gains and selflessness, we will only be drifting further and further apart.

You must learn to own up to your mistakes. You must be aware that you're not perfect. No one is. You are never going to be perfect, because no human will ever be perfect. We all make, and will continue to make, mistakes. Own. Up. To. Those. Mistakes. You must be a chameleon when it comes to anger and mistakes, which means to conform to your surrounding environment and see what you have done that is being viewed as a mistake. View it from their perspective. You must not get defensive when you're called out for making mistakes. Instead, own it, learn from it, grow from it, and don't repeat it.

For example: My wife and I recently were gifted a camp-er for use during the summer. We were excited to make some plans to get away a few times during the first few weeks of summer. My wife had the brilliant idea of doing a practice run up at her parent's property in a remote area of town north of us. Let me tell you, this practice run was a true blessing because we had a lot of situations that we had to deal with that helped us work together as a team, while showing us that when we work against each other, disas-ter strikes. I had ordered a tow kit for our brand-new SUV. The installation was canceled due to the manufacturing error of labeling the wrong kit with another one. There is a 3-week back order on the kit. My patience with their mistake, and not getting upset, was being rewarded with a free vehicle to use in order to continue our planned weekend. We had a few setbacks with repairs and preparation of the camper, but everything worked out. We arrived at my wife's parents' house. It had been raining most of the previous day and the ground was really saturated, so my wife suggested that we leave the camper in her parents' driveway for the night and move it in the morning. I stubbornly declined and ended up driving into the lawn and getting both the camper and the truck stuck. Her father was not at all happy with this outcome and frankly he didn't deserve my mishap hampering his weekend, by having to fix the damage of a now torn apart lawn. I was deflated. My wife felt defeated and wanted to return home. I was able to write this entire chapter based on this one event.

Although not angry with me, my father in-law wasn't happy about me ruining his lawn. I see him as a great man. He graciously cares for his family. I've learned a lot by just watching him move and live. One of the greatest pieces of advice he gave me was this: "People are not always happy. They are people and people always want more. So, when you do something and it's not to their liking. Fess up. Own it and don't complain about it. You got to fix it and move on." This was where my move forward in life moment/phase began, because I realized that I wanted and needed to change.

I noticed how defensive I got when anyone questioned me about anything. So I started to pray for change within me. I began to learn new ways to speak, being clear and precise in my intentions and responses. More importantly, I learned not to back away from mistakes, even the embarrassing ones. My in-laws have taught me patience, acceptance, love, appreciation and commitment. If there is one thing I can say was valuable, it's that they have also taught me about owning up to my wrong doings and thoroughly processing it in its entirety, so that it doesn't spread into other areas of my life. We must learn to fix what can be fixed and move forward with whatever we are working with in life. I'm truly grateful and I appreciate them both for that. Remember, own up to your mistakes and don't back away from them. Don't chase those mistakes, but move forward from them and learn to not repeat them. Listen. Watch. Learn. You must own up, to level up. This will eventually lead to a re-birth in you like never before and from the ashes of your past, you will be born again. Like. A. Phoenix.

CHAPTER 8
THE DEPTHS OF DEPRESSION

THE NEXT SUBJECT is a far more complex and sensitive one. Depression. Depression can be defined as: a mood disorder that causes a persistent feeling of sadness and loss of interest (Oxford Language). One of the biggest obstacles in a depressed person's life is self-doubt. We are going to explore this reasoning and map out a way to overcome depression and be the best you without having to rely on an outside source like pills.

In the Outer self, there is a universe of *you's* that struggle to gain control of your everyday activities. When your inner self is weak and virtually nonexistent, you most likely are a follower instead of a leader. However, you may be a follower in all aspects of your life. If you have a partner, they may be controlling and make every decision for you. You need this to feel functional. Even when it hurts you to your core, you refuse to leave. This would be your Outer self showing someone else that you want to be instructed and that you're weak minded. This becomes all you know.

Now the only thing that keeps you in balance is lost in the midst of being a follower. When you're lost, you're the opposite of what you once were and now your adverse self is in control for a short period. You do things you would never do, you act nothing like yourself. Everything about you is being erased over time and replaced with an empty feeling of you. You struggle each day, because you feel like you can never be a consistent version of yourself. Nothing makes you happy. You want to be around people, but when they arrive, you want nothing more than to be left alone and for everyone to go home. You have a hard time trying to make basic decisions in life, like what to eat or drink, or where to go for anything you need or want.

You have no idea why you're sad one moment and angry the next. Anxiousness and loneliness tend to surround you more than people do. This is the reality of a strong overcoming Apposite self. This part of you feeds on the dysfunction of the other three core parts. When you have a strong Apposite self, it's four times your normal self and therefore everything is magnified. This creates a feeling of never being happy again. The Apposite self thrives off the struggles of the other three core parts competing for dominance. This is where indecisiveness comes from. When you can't decide what to do, who you want to be, where you want to go or what you want to wear, your indecisiveness can give birth to a multitude of problems. But, what part of the personality does it start in and why?

The Outer self is made up of multiple versions of you. I explained this earlier: You have a multi-version of yourself. We all do. This does not mean everyone is bipolar, but rather a part of you that is different when you have encounters and interactions with people we know and meet in our life. It is the part of you shared with the people you know and love, the people you work with, and the people you encounter each day. You are also a different person each day you awake. How so? Nothing stays the same, and even though many of us have daily routines, there are too many variables for one to do the same thing, at the same time, with the same results, with every person, every single day. This is why it is impossible for you to be the same you day in and day out. You're consistently growing and your One Self is changing within. You must continue to process and move forward. Depression can cause these versions of you to be hurtful, closed off, or skeptical towards people and life. Researching and processing painful areas in your life can lead to the opening of many doorways to happiness and balance.

When I was a little boy, I had aspirations of living an independent, helpful life. My number one goal was to travel the world in 81 days and spread care packages to people in need. Well, where did that little boy go? Was he humbled? Is he now afraid? Did he die with his dream? I'm not the man I thought I'd be at this point in life. I for sure am not that little boy anymore. Life may throw curveballs, but many are there due to the decisions we make daily. Most of the curve-balls can be avoided. Selfishness is what makes us miss on the swing that would allow us to crush the curveball. Instead we strike out. Whiff! I come from a household of nine children. My father was a Christian. My mother was a Christian. Our lives were not built on a desire to accumulate material possessions, but on love, hard work and companionship. My father was a man who raised us hard. I got plenty of beatings for things I did wrong, and for wrongs I didn't do. I also think that sometimes the punishments were a lot more aggressive than the wrong that was committed.

My first memory is not a good one. I can remember everything about that moment and it made me resent my father for a long time when I was old enough to realize his way of upbringing was not how you raise a child. It's how you create monsters. I was definitely a monster. One that was made quietly for years. My first memory is of the very first time my father put his hands on me. It was a back handed smack that was so hard I could feel and smell the blood rushing through my nose. It was the first time I'd ever felt rage and anger. It would build with each hit. For years. In fact, my father only touched me affectionately once, in my entire life. That was when I returned home from boot camp. The second thing I'd ever completed in my life. He shook my hand and hugged me. Told me how proud he was of me. And that was that.

I held on to that anger. I swore I'd be a better father than he was. I swore that I would not become the man he was. People may have thought that my father was a man full of anger, regret and hatred for a lot of things in life. Maybe they thought he was a stubborn man or probably just a fool. My father was no fool. He is a very quiet and hard-working man. He did succeed in raising a fool of a son, though. His way of raising me was questionable. But I forgive him. I held onto that anger and tried not to be the part of him I hated, but ended up becoming just that. I was an angry man, full of rage and hatred for all things. I got angry at the slightest thing. I prayed for change and started to listen and learn. I began to preoccupy my mind with good thoughts and became more aware of myself, than at any other point in my life.

I was born as the youngest boy in my family, but the third youngest child of nine. My mother was a dear woman, who teamed up with my dad in their early years to provide the best that they could for their family. Now I am not saying we were dirt poor, but we were not living large either. Every penny counted. One of my earliest memories is of my folks reading to me out of this big white Bible that seemed like it was twice the size of me. We would read it as often as we could in those days. When I was about four years old, I noticed things starting to change around me. My parents always had pictures taken of us and I remember my dad telling me that my younger sister had a rash and bumps so bad on her body, that the photographer refused to photograph her. My dad, being of strong will, prayed and fasted and placed a small black hand Bible under her mattress each night and then the morning after he would pray. Now according to my father, when the photographer returned the following weekend, he thought that my parents were pulling a fast one on him and switched babies because her skin was smooth like that rash never happened. So clearly, religion was a big deal in my family.

My father was head of security for a large grocery chain in New York called Waldbaums. One day when I was about three, I was riding this tricycle. Man it was sweet...it was an all green Incredible Hulk tricycle complete with sound effects. I loved it as much as a three-year old could love (quite sure if I could have, I would have slept with it like a teddy bear). We lived in this three-story house and I was riding through the dining living room area when I saw my brothers heading down stairs and wanted to join them. So I followed...on my bike...down the stairs. Needless to say I injured myself pretty darn good. So "good" that my dad stayed home and was fired from his job in which he had given over eighteen years of his life too. He never really admitted it, but I think he secretly hated me for that. I remember his tone and look like it was yesterday. It will always be etched in my brain. A few days later I can recall what is the first bad memory I ever had. I remember my dad talking to my brothers about something that they were doing that needed to be changed. I remember my dad saying that now that he was out of a job things were going to be different--harder. He told my brothers that they might have to take on jobs to help out with the family. The conversation seemed to be directed towards the men so I walked out to join them, not to be nosy, just to be included and to be with the men in my family. Well, my dad didn't want that. Without warning he reached out and smacked me on my face. I remember the smell of blood and ringing in my ears. The stinging felt like my face was going to melt off. I remember him yelling, but I couldn't hear him as I raced back toward my room where I fell to the floor, blinded with fear of him. And as I lay there on the carpet looking back at him I felt lost and all I could think of was, "he'd miss me if I just left...I didn't even do anything!" It was at this moment that my extreme love for my father died. I was morbidly afraid of him after that.

Over the course of the next few years, my fear would grow with each hand that touched my face in that non affectionate way. I had rage that grew and grew. It would grow stronger with each slap of aggression. But, unknowingly my anger, aggression, fury, and rage were not against the one that started it. These feelings were against me. I hated myself, I hated life, I hated the fact that I had put my parents through whatever made them unhappy.

When I was twelve years old, we made a move from New York to Florida. I remember praying to God and thanking Him because I thought that I would and could have a new life in Florida. A life that would be free from the abuse, which I still felt responsible for. Right before the move, my dad was happier than I had seen him in years. He actually was getting dressed (from always being in pajamas), he even let us visit our friends before we left. After my dad lost his job, he fell into a deep depressive stage, that he never really got out of. He became a stay-at-home dad and felt the world was conspiring against him and his family. Race became a huge driver in his depression. Any rejection was because we were Black. Some of that may have been very true, but I'm not sure about all of it. So, him letting us go on adventures and to friends houses was a big welcomed change of pace. Much of the last few weeks were pretty fun.

One of the most exciting moments in my life happened during this time. It was when my two best buds and I found our teacher's name on the bronze stones that lined the Ellis Island shores to show the world who walked through Lady Liberty's gates to become Americans. We were all so excited to tell our teacher and he was so happy that he actually cried! When I got home I told my father and mother about the trip. For a small moment we shared something that made us happy and I saw a side of my father I was not used to seeing. He was happy. After that, my family started off on an adventure that would then change my life forever.

The move to Florida wasn't as good as I thought it would be. My dog died, my dad was always grumpy, our brand new garage door was vandalized, and all of this happened within the span of the first month. What a start to a new life, right? But this was where I noticed when my life changed, and not for the better. I was twelve years old about to turn thirteen. The next fifteen years would be the worst years of my entire life.

Life is very interesting and continuously developing. Learning to adapt to "your own" constantly changing life is the second most challenging thing one could face. Doing what is right and being a righteous person in God's eye is a hard thing to achieve. But trying to advocate feelings and emotions and staying out of worldly problematic situations that start out fun and almost always end chaotically, is harder than living a well scheduled and non-changing lifestyle. Now you have an imbalance of emotions that start to build on itself. At some point you may speak to a therapist or doctor that would say you were depressed and have a chemical imbalance and then they will treat you with some pills that will aid in adding balance and relief within you. I was once that person. The pills made me feel worse. It made life very painful and dramatic, and I felt abandoned by my family, my doctors and my friends.

I was a very lost individual. My little sister was very disappointed that I wasn't able to come home to take her to live with me once she graduated as I had promised her when I was younger. My mother was very sick and just a few short years from her eventual death. I lost my grandfather during that same year. I was married for six months and my wife was raped, then she cheated on me, and we got an annulment. We would also lose a child at birth in the middle of it all. I was harassed in my first career and lost all of my benefits. I was arrested quite a few times for driving without a license, just so I could earn a living. Bad choice, even though the situation that started it was not my fault, what caused the situation to go from good to bad was.

I spent countless nights losing sleep and suffering from it. I had lost all of my respect and trust from the people who knew me, because of my inconsistent nature and "get rich quick so I can be successful plans." I'd finally had enough with the inconsistency I created in my life and I decided that I needed to change. After much prayer, I just changed my entire approach on life. I forgave myself for the mistakes that I had made. I started out by making better decisions and being around better people that would hold me accountable for my actions, just as I would. This was not an overnight accomplishment, but rather months and years in the making.

The biggest thing I got out of all of this was trusting the process. God had a plan. Now that I knew that, I finally knew who I was and where I wanted to go. This would become the catalyst to a bigger and brighter future. I surrounded myself with good loving people. I was connected to a great church and a part of a trusting community. I followed all the things I've written about here, which is why I know that this works. I trusted God. I received and practiced patience, humility, gratitude, love and companionship. I got to a point where from the ashes of defeat and my burnt past old life, I was born again. Like. A. Phoenix.

CHAPTER 9
THE INSPIRATION FROM THE DEPRESSION

JULY 4TH, 2017. 10:08 AM. A white van is sitting at a red light in front of me. They have a series of letters applied to the rear of the van in a crooked line that read: "Do Something Amazing." It was like that was just left there for me to think about. What can I do that is amazing? Let me tell you this. If you have to *try* to be amazing, you will never be amazing. If you have to *try* and be phenomenal, you'll never be phenomenal. You don't try or train to be amazing or phenomenal, you just are. It's like when someone says, "This is going to be epic," or "This is going to be cool," and then it fails badly. Things aren't built or planned for epicness or coolness. They just happen to fall at the right times at the right moments with the right surroundings of places and people and it's just...epic. Don't try to be what you're not meant to be and in your own way, you *will* be cool, epic, and amazing.

I once heard Anthony Bourdain say, "I'm not afraid to look like an idiot." I embrace this notion, because anyone can be viewed as an idiot, just by breaking the mold of being normal. The Wright Brothers, Noah, Amelia Earhart, Martin Luther King Jr., Neil Armstrong, to name a few. It made me stop and think...

This is me.
One life, one love.
One chance, one opportunity.
To just be me. No matter what.
No matter how many doors may open.
Or close.
One life, one love.
One chance.
To be me.

To be viewed as an idiot, is to be seen. For me, that is a win. If you notice me, then I've interested you in who I am, and what I do. I'm going to always be me, if I do anything in this life, being me is what I will do best. It's the best thing I could ever own, and the only thing I will leave this earth with, if in fact we leave with anything. We must do away with the materialistic things we seek day to day. Let us instead enjoy ourselves and the company of each other. Make memories, create life, worship and grow into the next life that awaits us. Life is not about that "precious" stone you keep buried in your safe. It's not about the amount of money you have stored in your account. It's not the collectibles, or piles of items littering your homes and storage units because it might be worth something someday. We spend an amazing amount of time collecting things of no true value.

Example: You wake up in the morning laying on your box shaped bed, in your box shaped bedroom, in your box shaped home and go to your box shaped bathroom and take a shower in your box shaped shower. You grab your box shaped towel and head to your box shaped dresser to get your box shaped folded clothes before heading to your box shaped kitchen. You grab your box shaped food and then go to your box shaped parking spot, to get into your box shaped car, and drive down those box shaped streets to your box shaped jobs, at your box shaped desk. You earn your box shaped dollars, to fit in your box shaped wallets and purses, to buy more of your box shaped "needs." And yet, people will tell you that you need to think outside the box, and ask you to come up with round shaped ideas.

This is why pain can feel so capitalized at times. Society will tell you to keep your pain and get motivation from it. We are told to use pain as if it was a crutch, in order for us to become a better person. That is not what we should do, for those that do, it becomes a recycled element. You never move on from it. Just because someone, whether it's a friend, lover, or family member, tells you to use your pain as fuel for advancement or fire to be a better you, doesn't mean you have to agree with them on how you should use it. Embrace difference and new ideas that will open up your world to new adventures. Just don't forget who you are and what you value most. Your values, ideals and moralistic views may change or mature with time, but you can be prepared for that. Love yourself. Love your people. Love your values to your core and make those values good and not just values of materialistic things. Like pain, we must do away with the materialistic things we seek day to day and enjoy ourselves and the company of each other. We are building on a path to pursuing freedom.

Most of us may feel lost at times. Sometimes being lost is a great thing. It allows for travel. Travel within the One Self and that identity you seek to find. Travel the world for soil to settle upon. Remember, even those who have found themselves, find themselves lost. At times more often than others. Sometimes, finding ourselves means realizing and coming to grips with the knowledge of pain. For some of us, pain doesn't go away. Not just physical, but emotional pain. It seems like no one goes through more pain than those of us with a good heart. It's like, if we have a good heart, it sets us up to be hurt. Nevertheless, this does not give reason to close up and shut down, because at the end of the day, it's just emotional pain, and emotional pain is curable. A lot can be said of pain. My one take-away from a painful past is that if you actually take a moment and look back on your past, you'd see that much of it is self-inflicted pain by selfish and foolishly naive choices we have made. Think before you speak, leap, walk or run. Make good choices that will impact your future and the ones you love in more good ways than bad ways. For me, trusting in God by asking for His forgiveness and guidance and where He'd like me to go, was all I had for many painful nights spent alone. I learned to ask Jesus for grace and move forward. You must always remember that you must move forward.

We tend to keep pain as motivation. Put it right out in the trash and never come back for it. Pain is there to show you that whatever you're going through is real. It is a sense that something is not right and you need to fix it. Once you've received pain, you must reset yourself to get rid of it. If you're sitting next to a fire and an ember pops out onto your leg, you don't say "oh this hurts, but I'm going to tough it out and see if it goes away." No, you brush that thing off and move to a safer space. So, why then, do you put your emotional self through that trauma day in and day out? Pain can be hard to overcome. It also comes in many forms. Oh and guess what? At this very moment in your life, you've survived heartbreaks, traumas, devastation, failures, falls, breakups, losses, fights, accidents and turmoil. Yet, here you are still doing what you do best, rocking it by continuing to breath, read books and move on through life. You are awesome. You are amazing. You are epic. Do you see how being yourself can be an act of epic proportions? The key here isn't just to survive, but to get through the bad, swim to the good and realize that the bad is over. You made it and you did it. The key here is you shouting aloud, "I did it!" From the ashes of your very pain, you've emerged as a new you. Like. A. Phoenix.

CHAPTER 10
THE RENEWAL OF WITHIN

MY WIFE AND I had a huge fight one evening during the middle stages of writing this book. It was the busiest week of my year at work and I was trying to make sure that I had balanced my time between work and my wife. We spoke together and shared thoughts about our day and we watched shows together. Later that week my wife said she thought we'd had the crappiest week. It caught me off guard and I was subsequently offended. I was angered that my efforts were not acknowledged. I had once again, failed. We fought and I decided to continue to try and figure out our weekend. I was cutting the grass and went in to chat about that. She informed me that she was going to her mother's for the weekend. She'd never done this before. We didn't even talk about it like we used too. She left without saying goodbye and left a note on the table. That infuriated me. I noticed at the time this was my first clear cut feeling of complete anger and it felt like we were not going to be able to move forward from it. It felt like the end.

In hindsight my wife, being on the offensive side, called an audible, and removed herself out of the equation. This was in fact the best possible move she could make. It gave us time apart to process and level the situation. It allowed us to calm our nerves and recharge. It also helped me realize that I was stressed and irritated and needed a break.

We must allow our minds to wallow in small moments of silence throughout our days in order to figure out where we are at emotionally, physically and mentally. It is pivotal to the One Self. Enhance your mind by broadening your approach during down time. You will find that this rolls over into every relationship you are involved in. It will open up your mind to noticing which relationships are meant to be invested in, and which ones that need to be let go of. Listen you're not perfect. I get it, you want to please people and not let people down. But you don't need to befriend everyone you meet. You can make a person's day and move on without befriending them. There are risks involved in investing in people. Energy, love, time, and emotion. If none of those things are being reciprocated back by that person, it can destroy you. So choose wisely and listen. Rely on your heart and soul to tell you what your mind and flesh can't comprehend.

My wife and I have been continually doing things to "tune up" our relationship. We do something yearly if possible. Relationship tune ups are just like having mental times that allow you to recharge. They are vital anchors to ongoing relationships that will last a lifetime. Vacations, church outings, seminars are some examples of the things we do. This takes a lot of self-discipline. Self-Discipline can be defined as: the ability to control one's feelings and overcome one's weaknesses; the ability to pursue what one thinks is right despite temptations to abandon it (Oxford Language). One of my favorite quotes, is actually a bible verse:

> *For the spirit God gave us does not make us timid, but gives us power, love, and self-discipline.*

> — 2 Timothy 1:7.

You will never meet someone with all the same morals and principles you stand by. Even *you* don't agree with yourself all the time. That is what we call indecisiveness. This is something that we all have. Quit being so judgmental about who people. Don't fixate on what you're not. But rather who you are. You're not broken. You just don't know who you are yet. Identity and knowing who you are and where you want to be is a real struggle. Listen, I've fought through many tough times, where the only support I had was God, Jesus and the Holy Spirit. I've been through suicidal battles where death was the only outcome I could think of, and even tried to go through with it. Only to be saved or distracted by something that took my mind off of what I was currently lost in. I've been destroyed by women and friends to the point of being numb. Those experiences taught me to build up a wall against everyone. As soon as someone would get close, I moved away or destroyed what little friendship I had with them. There were an occasional few that got through the cracks.

But then one day, I was sitting alone and I suddenly realized I didn't like who I was. I didn't even know who I was. Let me tell you, that was a scary feeling. Finding myself was not an overnight transformation. In fact it's been a lifetime of continuous personal growth and smoothing out the edges. It's got to start somewhere. I'm not perfect and even though I'm striving to be a better me, I know I can never be perfect. I also know that I can't do it alone. I need the support structure of my community. My church. My work. My family. My friends. I've learned to talk and share my emotions at appropriate times. When I can't share, I've learned to separate and process those emotions and then return when I can. That may not work in all situations. That's okay, because that may be a point where you need to decide if it is healthy to continue on with the path in which that relationship may be heading.

Being suicidal and depressed is a very serious and strenuous. It is a dark, quiet and lonely place to be where the only voice you hear is your own. Everyone looks happy, and the grass is greener everywhere else. But if you were to start watering your own grass and begin planting new seeds, and allow it more light, your grass would be the greenest of pastures, and before long, you wouldn't really notice, or pay attention to any other grass. You're a pioneer. Pioneers need things to discover. Let that thing to discover be yourself, your life, and where it can take you. Let go of the weights that are bringing you down, release the chains of anger and animosity you have with the people of your past. There is a thin line between love and hate. Don't stand on the wrong side. That change has to start somewhere, so why not with you?

Change for me happened when I was getting out of jail from driving on a suspended license. I was at a friend's house on the outside of town. No car. No one to call. I decided to start my change with music. I would begin by only listening to Christian music when the radio was on. It started to reciprocate and replicate throughout my life. I still have battles and struggles. We always will. But now I have an army that walks with me and fights with me and guides me. Folks, life is going to be a battle. But when it is time to leave this Earth, let not one second have been wasted. Not a moment lost. Leave this Earth on E for empty. Give life everything you've got, every inch of yourself to being the best that you can be at all times. Make the lives of those around you so bright, that darkness will be a long forgotten past.

I once heard that the greatest place full of knowledge is the graveyard. It is there where you will find inventions, discoveries, ideas and dreams never brought to fruition. Mostly due to poor support and lack of trusting themselves to be able to achieve those dreams. Your biggest criticism comes from within and from those who surround you. Don't let that be a prison to stop you from achieving dreams and innovations. Break free from that place. A prisoner who's been set free is not called a prisoner anymore. This is a mindset in which we must place ourselves in more often in order to evolve. Evolution is very much a part of each of us. We evolve from embryo to newborn baby, to teenager, to adult to elderly and back into the ground from whence we came. That is the organic nature of our bodies. But our soul is totally different. We must continue to grow and learn and be hungry to do so. There is much in this world and in the next, that we need to learn.

> *Do not let your adorning be external—the braiding of hair and the putting on of gold jewelry, or the clothing you wear— but let your adorning be the hidden person of the heart with the imperishable beauty of a gentle and quiet spirit, which in God's sight is very precious.*
>
> — 1 Peter 3:3-4

Take a moment and review your life. What tedious things do you have or do that can be set aside, so that you can put full focus on your goals? What new things can you learn?

Remember, don't be a prisoner of tediousness. Be a defender of yourself and the goals laid before you. Like a rubber band, hold those together and combine those into one great moment of life. In its simplest form a rubber band is just that, a rubber band, but what it can be is a holder or combiner of things. And when you stretch that rubber band, you introduce tension. That tension now becomes what that rubber band is. Remember the difference of what life is and what life *can* be. So remember that your past obligations can make you a prisoner that is struggling within your One Self. You're free from those. If they still have you, you should pray. You must see that you are set free from the old ways of your old self because a debt, your debt, has been paid. The ransom for your life has been claimed and you're free. Remake yourself from the ashes of defeat and allow the love of Christ Jesus to set you anew and free! Like. A. Phoenix.

Jesus is a part of my life. This book exists because God and Jesus gave this to me to write. Each year at New Year's, I had a voice that would say, "knock, knock, you should write a book," and each year it was never written. It got started once many years ago, but never finished. Until now. God dropped that book on me like sunshine on a meadow. And I was lit with a fire like never before to complete something. I had a two year commitment that was exceeded by writing the first draft in seven months. That is a miracle! This was a gift given to me. I'm just a vessel for it to go through.

For the word of God is living and active, sharper than any two-edged sword, piercing to the division of soul and of spirit, of joints and of marrow, and discerning the thoughts and intentions of the heart.

— Hebrews 4:12

I've had many Jesus moments. Two or three of them were lifesaving and or life changing events like being hit by a car as a kid, being involved in or witnessing near fatal car accidents in California, where I shouldn't have walked away, having suicidal moments where the unquestionable miracle prevented me from ending what would later become a beautiful life. I say this so that if you need help, pick up your phone and call the Suicide Hotline in your area. Search for a church near you. Go sit at a service and seek fellowship and companionship and become a follower of Jesus. If you want to be a follower of Jesus, pray these words with me.

Dear Lord **Jesus**, I know that I am a sinner, and I ask for Your forgiveness. I believe You died for my sins and rose from the dead. I turn from my sins and invite You to come into my heart and life. I want to trust and follow You as my Lord and Savior.

Welcome to the family, my friend. Now let's be born again. Like. A. Phoenix.

CONCLUSION

MY PURPOSE IN writing this book was twofold. To learn more about myself in the context of doing a project and to give hope to people who feel overwhelmed by their past or their current struggles. For me, my faith background is my strength. The standard God has for us is perfection and it's often discouraging to know that you will never be "good enough." Instead of focusing on that, remember the promises God has given to us. He promised to send his Son, and He did. He promised His Son would die, and He did. He promised His Son would rise from death, and He did. He promised that our sins would be forgiven, and if you accept Christ and follow Jesus, they are. The promises of God are amazing and the only thing that keeps us going in times of disappointment. Christians get the opportunity to experience joy despite our suffering. We get the opportunity to grow in love, grace, hospitality, and many other character traits of Jesus as we learn more and more about Him.

It won't be uncommon for us to go back and visit stories that we've already touched on and go into more detail, and process what has happened in order to obtain growth. But it is also common for us to move on and never look back on situations, but rather create new fond memories of the days and moments with loved ones. Our trials, tribulations and testimonies are probably vastly different from any other persons, and that is okay. It is why life is commonly referred to as: the book of life. Although I hope you walk away from this book realizing that no one person's story is better than another's, that is not the reason we are here on this planet. We don't become beautiful. We are beautiful. Each and every one of us. It's time for us to show the world what true beauty is, in the realest form. Ourselves.

The thing to be recognized as the most important thing is that you are constantly trying to get closer to the God who loves you and are in a trusting community of believers where you can be transparent about your struggles and have people pray with you and over you. You're not the center of it all. Trust the process and move forward. Always remember to keep moving forward. God has a plan. Even in your many mistakes you'll make (because you have a choice in all that you do) in life, if you trust the process, you'll get there. Things are not going to be easy because you trust God and pray to Jesus. You still have to work. But having a support structure and courage does make it easier to move forward. If you're in the right place in life. When you get there, burn off the habits of the old you, and be born again from the ashes, and like a phoenix, take flight and fly. Fly high over the mountains and prevail, as the beautiful creature that you are. Like. A. Phoenix.

As I pace in this life, I've found myself faced with a "Good Will Hunting" moment. Why will I be considered a laughing stock, because I wrote about something with no background? Do I really need to have a degree to be thought of as educated? Libraries and books exist where teachers do not. Life is also one of the greatest books a person can read. My people, my friends, life is background. It is experience. For some, it is love. I write because I see. I see because I feel. I feel because I listen. I listen because I love. We always come full circle. From the ground we came, to the ground we return.

God is a powerful God. His love, grace and patience, is challenged by nothing and no one. My life has been and will continue to be hard. But, when I gave it all to God, something happened. A peace grew within me. Within those limits, everything seemed possible. My people, my friends, find this. Find this love, this peace. It will resonate with you forever. Do not let this world control what is meant for you to do. We are meant to love, learn, feel and heal. Make no mistake, with feeling comes pain. This life we live is full of it. But the next life is pure joy and love. The four parts of you that we all share, need balance, compassion, grace and room to grow. Feed your soul, feed your mind. Love yourself and love others. Never forget who put you here to do what you were born to do. Until next time...

— ZXN Natallanni

ACKNOWLEDGEMENTS:

I WANT TO THANK God first and foremost. Without Him, this book doesn't exist. When you pray things do actually happen. But work comes with that, and it takes a village to make dreams happen and become true. My mother Julie, my wife Marie, my Pastor Jason Deuman, my friend Chris Lyons. There are so many more.

Additionally, the 100 Seeds of Promise, 13th & Joan and its founder Ardre Orie and Cami were each inspirational in the development of this piece. This is only the beginning ladies and gentlemen. God has work that needs to be done. Let's continue our efforts to make this work be done.

> *2 Corn 5:7*
> *For we walk by faith, not by sight.*

CPSIA information can be obtained
at www.ICGtesting.com
Printed in the USA
FSHW020504110821
83862FS

9 781953 156266